One year of Poetry

2022 – 2023

A Poetry Anthology
Edited by
Lis McDermott

LIS' POETRY PLACE

Lis' Poetry Place is an online group of poets who have met during the last two years. Some members have come and gone, but these are the core members for this year.

Led by Lis McDermott, we meet monthly to share the poems written during the month by group members; share poems by other poets, introducing the group to poets perhaps previously unheard, and we explore different poetry forms.

Group members are all at different stages in their poetry journey. For more information please see the information at the end of the book.

https://lismcdermottauthor.co.uk/poetry-place.html

CONTENTS

Each section is made up of a group of poems written for specific prompts set throughout the year.

Individual poets responded in their own styles, to the prompts reacting to their personal feelings about the subject matter.

Each Poets' Bio can be found on page **143**

SONGS

ELEANOR RIGBY

Eleanor Rigby, living her best life,
With friends aplenty, and a new wife.
Father Mackenzie has no funerals to do.
He only does weddings, and a christening,
or two.

There are no lonely people, living in dingy
flats,
And everyone has a dog or a cat.
There's always something nice to see,
And always somewhere you have to be.

Eleanor Rigby, in love with her new wife,
And Father Mackenzie has no strife.
There are no lonely people, where have
they all gone?
Imagine if this had been their song!

Fiona Oliver

A HOUSE IS NOT A HOME

The perfect house, having the perfect view,
full of happy children spreading their
wings,
appears to be the wish for homely bliss.
Over years, dreams and plans can go
askew.
Growing apart, aim for different things,
with few shared memories to reminisce.

To arrive home and be greeted by thee
each day; your bright eyes would make my
heart sing
as you hold me close to impart your kiss;
To live in a home without love would be
remiss.

Lis McDermott

YELLOW TAXI

Big yellow taxi parked on the street,
Sun kissed sidewalks, hazy with heat.
Central Park rowing boats meander their
way.
New York, at its finest on a hot Summer's
day

But look a little closer and you will see,
It's not all milk and honey, in the land of
the free.
At the steps of the library, holding a sign,
Is a veteran begging for a dollar or dime.

There's graffiti which tells its own grim
tale,
Of broken lives, and dreams that have
failed.
The sunshine seems a little less bright,
When you're down and out, and you've
lost the fight.

Paradise, has sadly been paved,
And parking lots are used for raves.
We still don't know what we've got till it's
gone,
But we know life was better when Joni
wrote her song.

Fiona Oliver

LIFE, LOVE AND LOSS

RULES FOR MY LIFE

Always buy good underwear
Don't take the lift, use the stairs!
Cheap loo roll is a waste of money!
Start your day with toast and honey.
Love your family, hold them dear.
Try new things, fight your fears.
Stay in touch with your friends.
Don't keep buying new books and pens.
Eat when you're hungry and savour it.
Accept you're never going to be super fit!
Respect others and yourself.
Always protect your mental health.
Live, love and laugh a lot
Tell your husband he's blooming hot!
Never let anyone put you down
Try and smile, and not to frown
Write poetry and make art
Don't wait to tomorrow, make a start!

Fiona Oliver

RULES FOR MY LIFE

I decided long ago
That rules were made to break
And so today I tell you all
Don't make the same mistake.

Your life is yours to live the way
You want it just to be.
And so, you should set out those rules
For one and all to see.

My rules are very simple.
I decided this long ago
I'll live my life to suit just me
If you don't agree, well blow!

Ann Brady

WILL YOU?

If I am sad and feeling down
because of all my life-ly woes,
and I feel the world is wrong
Will you try to comfort me?

If it rains and spoils the day
destroying all my well laid plans
upon which my happiness relies
Will you come and save the day?

If I feel the need to laugh
But cannot find a reason why
I should even try to smile
Will you tell a joke to me?

If my eyes start to cry
Water running down my cheeks
Sadness enveloping me
Will you kiss and wipe my face?

When I feel a need for love
Not knowing why I may feel scared,
Knowing you are not there
Will you come and rescue me?

When you have left this earthly world
And I sit here all alone
Needing, wanting only you
Will I remember all you've done for me?

Ann Brady

DO YOU KNOW LOVE YET?

My father came to me last night,
Though he has long since passed away.
Three times he's been to ask of me
So, I knew what he would have to say.

His figure full of love, though stern
Stood at the bottom of my bed.
'Do you know love?' he asked of me
'Of course, I do' I said.
'I've been in love so many times.'
Despairingly, he shook his head

'I cannot keep on coming back
Until you really know
What loving others truly means,
Then you can let my spirit go.'

And after many years went by
I lived through joy and often pain,
When finally, I understood,
My father came again

'We learn to love the lives we touch
　　Whether they be good, or bad,
　　We care for those who need our help
　　Some happy souls, some sad.'

'But does love sometimes have to hurt',
　　　　I asked.
He smiled, 'My time with you is done,
　　But yes, it often does,' he said,
'Like a fathers' love, for his wayward son'.

John Phillips

THE LONELY HEARTS CLUB

Have you a lonely heart like mine?
Can I provide the loving care you
constantly pine?
I'm a retired widow, still young at heart, an
amateur
dramatic fanatic, sporty too, playing
bridge, golf and tennis.
A solvent owner of my own home, who's
smart and conscientious.

Seeks a genuine gentleman in his sixties,
living in the Brighton area with similar
interests to mine, who desires to form a
loving relationship too.
Could this be you?

Initially meeting for outings, theatre,
romantic dinners for two,
and perhaps more;
Life is a mystery, who can tell what else
may be store?
Please send your details, with a photo to
Box No. 124.

I'm an ex-army officer who proudly served in the Afghan task forces.
A widower, owner of two dogs and three racehorses.
I'm seeking a well healed, upper-class, attractive,
flamboyant filly in her thirties, early forties, with no ties
for fun, wining, dining and socialising with the Surrey County set.
Must be a horse racing lover, a good each way bet.
If you feel you are qualified, contact me with a photograph and details of pedigree to Box No. 33.

Are you all alone, just like me?
Is travelling the world something you hope to foresee?
Can I make your dreams come true?
If you have time to spare, come join me on a sensational world cruise for two.
No strings attached, all for a competitive fee;

It will be an amazing adventure, just wait and see.

Imagine climbing up Mr Eiffel's monumental tower:

Visiting Japan when the cherry blossoms are in full flower:

See the famous Sydney Opera House as you sail into the harbour:

Buy a hot dog in Time Square served by a genuine New Yorker:

Sit on a beach in Tahiti, sipping cocktails in style:

Watch a magnificent sunset on Egypt's great river Nile.

Don't delay, time and tide wait for no man.

All arrangements are in hand.

Both male and female applications considered.

Age range 40 to 65.   Contact Box No. 999.

A distinguished, middle aged MP from Essex,

Desperately seeks a distraction after recent parliamentary hysterics.

Desires to meet a fun-loving lady for friendship,
who enjoys socialising and partying frolics.
Candidates should be aged between twenty and thirty.
Preferably will be fit and sporty;
As well as being attractive, blonde, slim it's essential
you are of good character and honest.
Future good times are sincerely promised.
If you fit the bill, you know the drill, send a photograph,
together with resume to Box No.10.

Carolyne Crawford

I LIVED, I LOVED

As I sit in my window staring at the busy
world
All I see are passing strangers far too busy
to care about me.
In this room of isolation, surrounded by
those things of mine
I wonder what my life would have been
like,
If only I had never loved.
When young you think that romance is
genuine,
It's what true love is all about.
And yet, as the years pass slowly by,
you realise it's all just been a lie.
For now, as I sit staring at the strangers,
wondering if they will ever love,
Or will they too become as lonely, as this
woman sat in the chair?
No one knows that I was famous, no one
knows the life I've led.
Yet only I can tell these strangers of all the
joys that I've felt.

And so, I sit here in my window, dreaming
of my life now past.
For in my world I was a woman, who
loved, and lived her very best.

Ann Brady

TAKE WINGS AND FLY

My hope our love lasts forever
a love, that no-one can sever.
Filled with such joyous love, I lift,
take wings and fly.

I dream, wish, even pray on high,
thank the gods for a love so pure.
My hope our love lasts forever,
take wings and fly.

Even after death I will lie,
shed feathers deep in your mem'ries.
Together, hearts entwined we will
take wings and fly.

Lis McDermott

TRUE LOVE

'How many times have you been in love?'
I asked an old family friend of mine.
He counted slowly as he spoke their names,
Then said- 'I do believe that's nine'.

I did not expect it to be that many
And blurted out 'That seems a lot'.
He smiled and said 'Please listen to me,
Then you will understand, it's not.

You should always respect the lady you're
with
as it is something she will always
remember,
Even if only a summer romance
you both know will end come September.

To say- I love you- is easy
You hear it so often in song,
But to be, *in love*, is magical
and the feeling you get, will go on.

You should never break a lover's heart,
As a woman's love is a treasure.
She should always recall what you meant
to her,
as a time in her life that was pleasure.

So, you may want girlfriends while still a
youth,
to flirt and have some fun.
But you will never regret, simply being in
love,
many times, as I have done'.

John Phillips

A GRANNIES LOVE

I will still be with you Christmas morn
As you gather round the tree
And watch as you unwrap your gifts
There'll be one there from me

You cannot see or touch it
But you will feel it in your soul
It is my everlasting love
That I leave there for you all

No longer can you see me
Sitting in my old armchair
But as long as you can feel my love
You will know I'm always there.

John Phillips

YOUR NATIVE SON

Remember me this time of year
As with you now I cannot be,
For I have left my life behind
In distant lands you'll never see.

I'm still the child that went away,
And I was someone's dad,
I was the husband that you loved,
The brother that you had.

My body's wounds no longer heal,
I can no longer feel the pain.
The only hurt that that I would feel
Is if in time, you lose my name.

For medals and glory I did not care,
Only duty and family, the reason why
I gave my life as I was asked,
These are the reasons that I die.

But there is one thing for which I care,
And it is not much, that I ask done.
Please, never let my memory die,
Remember me always, your native son.

John Phillips

FOR DARCY

You always sat there by my side
Comforted me on a lonely night
To guard me, and protect me,
With all of your tiny feisty might.

I thought that we would both grow old
Together, you and me.
What was to come, I could not know,
Your life cut short, I could not see.

Never again do I want to love,
Or even do I want to care.
The memories of you hurt too much,
I still look for you, knowing you're not
there.

You looked at me with trusting eyes
I swear I saw you smile.
I'd give up days of my own life
To walk with you, for one more mile.

This is not how I imagined
how our journey would end.
You hid your pain from me so well,
my faithful, precious friend.

You still looked like a pup to me
So, was I wrong to let you go?
Did you have left, just a little more time?
It's too late now; I'll never know.

John Phillips

HOME

My children have all grown up
The family nest they've flown
My soul-mate long since passed away
So now I live here on my own.

All of my friends have moved away
They say they'll keep in touch
'We'll come and visit you, someday
We love you very much'

But no one seems to call to chat
Or even share a pot of tea
The phone it doesn't ring so much
I think they've all forgotten me

I'm greeted by an empty house
No one to say 'how was your day
A mirror is my company
But he does not have much to say

I own a house
But it's not a home
As I now live here
All alone.

John Phillips

FROM YOUR SON

I stood beside you yesterday
When you laid flowers on the ground
And watched you weep, now openly
As there was no one else around.

It saddens me that you still grieve,
Since so much time has come to pass.
Have faith, believe, the son you loved
Has never lain beneath the grass.

At my photo you stare, every single day
I hear you talk to it at night,
With joyless eyes you look again
When you awake with dawns new light.

Please Dad, you need to understand,
There is no need for you to mourn.
I had to shed my mortal shell,
Or else I could not come back home.

But time will pass, and then one day
Your spirit also will be free,
Returning where we all came from,
Then once again, you'll be with me.

John Phillips

THE DARKNESS

I dread the dark nights
The very short days
With fading light
limited sun rays
It's the dark that I dread

I dread the dark days
Feeling the cold
With a fire ablaze
Waiting for warmth
Someone to hold
It's the cold that I dread

I dread the dark feelings
That seem to take hold
As I gaze at the ceiling
As the cold takes hold

It's the loneliness I dread
A love long gone
Alone in my bed
Will I make dawn?
It's the feeling of dread, I dread

Debra Pitchford

DEEP AND DARK

Deep dark sin stays hidden within,
eating you from inside out
crawling just beneath your skin,
causing you to suffer doubt.

Deep dark sin stays hidden
forever in your heart,
cold, soulless, amongst men
sets you from them apart.

Deep dark sin stays
hard to conceal,
like a malaise
unfit to heal.

Deep dark
black, evil sin
upon you makes its mark.
Deep dark sin stays hidden within.

Lis McDermott

LOST

I have lived so many lives before
All of the happy ones with you
But then our soul, a single love
The universe split into two

How long am I doomed, to search this
world?
As on my own I'm not meant to be
Will I ever find what I'm looking for?
Or will there always be, just half of
me

So many times, I have been reborn
Each time I know I am not whole
How can I be when I have lost?
The best part of my soul

I'll wander through a life once more
Knowing that I'm incomplete
And pray that destiny be kind
For my soul mate once again to meet.

John Phillips

DEEP DARK SIN

We all possess deep, dark sin,
Sin that holds us captive, lying hidden in
mysterious depths within.
Re-emerging at any time, to torment with
guilt and shame, at an ungodly whim.
The addictive power of sin perpetuating,
again, and again.
We live in a world where jealousy, hate,
deceit are the order of the day.
It was only 'a little white lie,' people say.
That's not how life was intended to be,
We were created to be caring, to live good
lives, born to be free.
To experience hope, feel joy,
Not to be lost to sin, that's quick to
destroy.
No-one is immune to sin and temptation,
Life hurts, everyone falls short of heavenly
perfection.
Transform hate into loving kindness,
Break the chains of sin that bind us.
Don't battle or fight, make peace, not war.

Banish deceit and lies, the truth to restore.
Try to do what is good and right, in God's
holy sight.
Sin ruins lives, relationships, is it wise to
remain locked, in this dreadful plight?

Carolyne Crawford

MEMORIES

NOT THE LAND OF MY FATHERS

All though the day was overcast
we went out for a drive.
Along we went, across and up the valleys
green,
until we reached the sky.

It's strange, how sights, sounds and smells
bring old memories back to life.
The way our ancestors lived their lives?
Sometimes happy, yet often full of strife.

It was the green of the climbing hills
and the cobbled stone terraced houses,
that made the thoughts of ages past rise
into visions before my very eyes.

I searched my mind to discover,
thoughts of relatives long since passed,
I knew that they would be at home
living and working in the places we did
pass.

For though I am a Yorkshire Lass
and proud of my county home,
my kinship also belongs right here
in these valleys that we did roam.

It made me think of the working men,
whose lives were spent down in the dark
confines.
Yet, so it was for my kith and kin who
were
working in the South Yorkshire Coal
mines.

So, even though I'm Yorkshire bred.
A Yorkie through and true.
I'll place my hand upon my heart, to
swear allegiance to this here Wales too.

Ann Brady

MY LEGACY

His heart was big, his legacy was greater,
He started life as a lowly decorator.
Times were hard, people were poor;
He was renowned for being a hard-worker
that's for sure.

Never wishing for fame or wealth,
Always thinking of others before himself.
His first priority in life was caring for
his daughters and wife.

Cycling miles for work, through lashing
rain, on his rickety old bike.
Working long shifts to keep his family
clothed, fed and warm.
My father, my hero, my friend, my first
port of call in a raging storm.

When fortunes improved, he'd happily
give you his last penny, if he could.
He was an old-fashioned, honourable,
gentleman, who fought for his country,
was brave and good.

His legacy of love and selflessness
is locked away deep inside my heart;
Death was the only thing that could
keep us apart.

Carolyne Crawford

STUDENT MEMORIES

Hearing James Taylor sing, 'You can close
your eyes'
I'm transported in a milli-second, back to
1971
Sitting in my college room, bright, yellow,
poster-full walls,
Wherever have those years gone?

Bass line of a rock anthem booms through
from the boys next door,
Creating a mix with the music in our
house, adding a discordant air.
Art students upstairs, dreaming, high, waft
down *herb* aromas,
They are rumbled regularly by the police,
which doesn't seem fair.

Long flowing skirts, long hair, flared jeans,
and smock tops,
dressed in Mums' back-in-style old fur
coat, I feel upbeat,

Piano music, heavy in my home-made
purple, blanket bag,
I flounce along the street, smiling at
everyone I meet.

In my first week, of the first year, I met
Norman,
Three years spent together, having fun and
leading each astray,
Yet, firm friends we became, never lovers.
Fifty-three years on, our friendship remains
to this day.

It's true! Those were some of the best days
of my life,
Listening to Sweet Baby James' gentle
tenor voice,
Preparing college work, for next day's
lecture….
I smile at the memories, causing my heart
to rejoice.

Lis McDermott

THE SKIPPING NEEDLE

'Your house is so untidy,'
My mother always said.
At least it's quiet now these days
Since she is a long time dead.

I hated all her visits.
Her complaints about my mess.
She didn't remember her childhood
Or causing her mother any stress.

That's because she was Miss Perfect.
Who always got it right?
I bet she was so brilliant,
as she and her sister didn't fight.

But I remember why it was untidy
and why I was so primal.
I always had the sewing out with
the falling needle skipping over the vinyl.

I hated those days of frustration
until I finally did say shut up.
I found a Holly Hobby Poster
which became my favourite pin-up.

You see it said 'this house may be untidy
But no matter where you roam,
you should always try and remember,
that it's clean and it is a home.

Ann Brady

THE OLD OAK DOOR

Peeking around the high unkempt hedge;
She discovers a quaint, old fashioned, thatched
cottage up ahead.
At first sight, truth be told, the whole place
looks in disrepair, requiring hard-work,
loving care.
The old cottage exudes a sense of sadness,
despair.
Like a jungle the garden lay in ruins all
around;
Where once pretty hollyhocks, delphiniums
grew
tangles of prickly brambles, weeds creep
unchecked along the ground.
Ancient bushes, plants grow spindly, wild
in their brave attempt to survive.
Despite the straggling, overgrown mess,
the old cottage
has charm enough, with expert help, to
come alive.
To her surprise, behind a rambling briar
rose she spies
a particularly beautiful, worn proud with
age, old oak door.

Welcoming, inviting her to enter, come inside, explore.
Her imagination takes flight, if the door could speak what
tales of bygone times would it impart;
Memories of families from the past, their loves, sorrows,
dreams, of painful, broken hearts.
How many blushing brides, lovingly held in strong arms
were carried through the old, creaky door?
Would it tell of the heartbreak, anguish of bereft families,
mourning loved ones lost in war, on a foreign shore?
Was it Destiny calling her onwards to explore?
In anticipation, she proceeds on inside to discover what
treasures lay in store,
Hidden out of sight, behind the beautiful, old oak door.

Carolyne Crawford

GONE BUT NOT FORGOTTEN

The coal my Uncle dug, he daily burnt as
by the fireside he sat.
His wife wanted to leave her lonely life,
but fate prevented her from doing that.
Their daughter's accident being severe,
they lived in their united prison of fear.
My other Uncle laughed, was full of joy,
but his life the cancer it did destroy.
The woman who gave me grandmotherly
advice, waited for her first-granddaughter,
until then her life was not to be sacrificed.
My mother, who in the last years of her
life, reconciled with her forgotten eldest
child.
These are just a very few, of the people I
once knew.
Now that they have left this domain, only
my memories are all that remain.

Ann Brady

ON THE BRIGHT SIDE

MILO THE DOG

It was a momentous day when Milo the
puppy
came to stay.
What a great life being on a pet merry-go-
round of
eating, sleeping, having fun, 'walkies' and
play.
Milo is friendly, lovable and bright,
With his big floppy ears, large brown
eyes,
golden curly coat; it was love at first
sight.
You could see he was going to be big by
the size
of his paws.
When teething, Milo was famous for
gnawing at the
skirtings, scratching the doors.
Very soon he was adopted into the family
as
'one of the boys'.
Although, heaven forbid if the cat ever
tried to eat
his food, or share his toys.

Mum suffered from shock when Milo started thieving
their socks,
For eating paper hankies, he's also renowned.
Bounding around in nearby fields is where he   loves
to be found,
Madly galloping at great speed, chasing leaves,
retrieving his old, battered ball.
He's growing up fast to be lanky and tall.
Out and about his bark is worse than his bite,
Chasing cats, squirrels is his favourite delight.
Smaller pooches in fright often turn tail, run the
opposite way,
Alas, poor Milo only wants to be friends, and play.
Life is never boring when Milo the mischievous
Golden Doodle is out on patrol,
scampering, barking,
sniffing inside and out, around and about.

Carolyne Crawford

CHRISTINE DAY

Christine Day on her mobility scooter
Drives so fast and has no hooter,
On the pavement and on the streets
Driving straight at all she meets.

Kids and grannies fall like trees
And she's cut some off at the knees.
Just two speeds - stop and go,
Braking's not her style you know.

She loves to make people jump and cry,
And one day they may even fly -
Through the air as she barrels past,
She drives so very, very fast

But one day she'll hit a large pot hole
And this will surely take its toll.
Her mobility scooter will be no more
And we'll all be safer, that's for sure.

So, Christine, please have some care,
You crazy, super speedy, mare!
Reign it in and show some skill,
Before you make your first road kill.

Fiona Oliver

ODE TO SWEET DELIGHTS

I can see them on the sideboard, like soldiers
on parade standing there all in a row.
Offering tantalising promises of the wonderful
joy they'll very soon bestow.
I could easily eat one in five minutes flat;
at the drop of a hat.
But no, I knew they were off limits, it was crystal
clear there were consequences should I show
greedy intentions, touch or venture too near.
The agony of temptation was too heavy a burden
to bear, I fear.
Silently they taunted me to devour one and all,
Waiting for the last of my weak defences to fall.
They looked deliciously pretty,
individually

wrapped in colourful silver paper, in a
beautifully
beribboned cardboard box.
If I'd been as quiet as a mouse, or sly like a
fox,
Perhaps I could've spirited one away to
eat,
before anyone noticed in our house.
Could anyone resist the addictive qualities
of such
delightful, melt in the mouth tasty
confectionery?
The sweetest of treats, that ultimately is the
cause
of divine taste bud ecstasy.
I'm sure the calorific value is truly
extraordinary.
When buying Easter Eggs for the
grandchildren,
I recall, with great fondness, those childish
days
of sweet, chocoholic fantasy.

Carolyne Crawford

MY NIGHT BEFORE CHRISTMAS

Not a creature was stirring
Not a sound in the house
As we had finally caught
That dam squeaking mouse

My fat slob of a stepdad
Was asleep in his chair
Still wearing booze soaked pyjamas
He just didn't care

He was mums' latest husband
I think number four
But for my gin-sodden mother
There will be several more

Then a noise from the kitchen
Such a terrible clatter
She had dropped the cooked turkey
But said "it don't matter"

With a fag in her mouth
She just staggered about
"Just phone the Chinese
And we'll have a take-out"

As once more in our house
Christmas eve looks like shite
I am off down the pub
Where I can have a good night.

John Phillips

TORNADO IN THE ATTIC

(A VISIT FROM THE 3 BEARS)

They said the house was haunted
but I thought that they did jest.
Until the night the noises started
disturbing me from my rest.

Did I have an unwanted intruder?
A rat or mouse giving me a scare?
Maybe it was some big large bird
fluttering about everywhere.

Perhaps, a ghostly haunting,
from ghouls, earthly bound.
The sounds were like a tornado,
with furniture being tossed around.

Boxes were scattered from side to side,
Yet a rat or mouse were not so strong,
to move a sideboard six feet wide
across a loft so large and long.

So, what was making the horrible noise?
It sounded like a raging goose,
I was too scared to go and look
in case a wild cat had gotten loose.

I packed a case and rang my friend.
"Quick, come and rescue me."
But when she went to investigate,
She laughed loudly as can be.

"You silly girl," she told me.
"No wonder you escaped down the stairs".
You'd left the loft window wide open,
So inside are three friendly bears."

It's time for us to move them on,
then we'll tidy up, and take stock.
"Now relax for the bears have gone,"
said my dear friend, Miss Goldilocks.

Ann Brady

SPRING

I've been coiled tight, hibernating.
Lethargic, listless, procrastinating.
I've lingered in the wintry gloom,
but I'm so ready for Spring to bloom.

I'll wash the car, and then the cat.
Dust the shelves and beat the mat.
I'll clean the windows, and the doors
catch the cobwebs, steam the floors.

I'll lose a stone, maybe two.
Take up yoga, and Pilates too.
I'll shave my legs, buy fake tan.
Paint my toe nails, if I can.

I'll paint my bedroom, buy a new bed,
or maybe change the kitchen instead.
I'll power wash the patio,
plant some flowers, watch them grow.

I'll try new things, learn to cook,
maybe try and write a book.
I'll walk ten thousand steps a day,
Invite my family to stay.

I'll take my vitamins and dig deep,
How will I fit in eight hours of sleep?
I'll have a think about this all
Wake me up when it's the Fall.

Fiona Oliver

WHAT HAPPENED TO YOUR WINGS?

Whatever's happened to your wings?
You're covered in dust and other things.
You look like you've been through the mill.
Are you broken, are you ill?

Whatever's happened to your wings?
Was it the slide? Maybe the swings?
Your hair is messed up, full of dirt
And there's a hole in your skirt!

Whatever's happened to your wings?
And where's your wand, and all your bling?
Your glittery heels have lost the fight
Oh dear me, you look a sight!

Whatever's happened to your wings?
You're bouncing - like your feet are springs!
What a party it must have been…
You're the wonkiest fairy I've ever seen!

Fiona Oliver

MOTHER OF THE BRIDE

My gorgeous girl is getting married
I'm so proud, but also harried!
No bridal tantrums from my girl
It's me, whose feeling in a swirl!

What to wear on this special day,
what to do, and what to say?
Shift dresses are not my bag
and bolero jackets make me gag.

I'm not a super skinny mum
I've got a large and curvy bum,
It's hard to find a perfect frock,
Larger sizes, always out of stock!

I'm wide of shoulder and of hip,
Maxi dresses make me trip,
Plump knees, rule out a mini,
Can't wear my PJ's or my pinny!

I've found a frock I quite like,
even if it's rather tight!
I've bought a corset to make me
thinner,
I can't breathe, but I'm looking
slimmer.

I need a hat with a deep brim,
and my hairy legs will need a trim.
Hair and make -up will help a bit,
but what if my dress bursts, when I sit?

I've bought six spare dresses, just in
case,
And I'm doing Pilates, to shrink my
waist.
I'm under pressure, eight weeks to go.
I must hydrate, I need to glow!

I'm a bag of nerves, but my girl's cool,
Elegant and so beautiful.
In saner moments, I unwind
There are six tall bridesmaids, I'll hide
behind!

Fiona Oliver

WEATHER MAN

The weather man said trust me, it won't
rain.
My trust was given, but all in vain!
No umbrella, or coat with a hood,
Wet through to my knickers, there I stood.

The doctor said trust me, you won't feel a
thing.
My trust was given, there would be no
sting.
The jab was needled into the top of my
arm!
The air turned blue, it caused some alarm!

The fraud team said trust us, we're your
bank
You've been a victim of fraud - it stank!
Give us your PIN number, we are the real
deal…
And all my money, they did steal!

The website said trust us, it's true to size
Fashion houses never lie!
Our one size only will fit you all …
Even if you're short or tall!

The bungee team said trust us, we've got you!
As I finally jumped - what a view!
They trusted me to give my actual weight
And now it seems, it's all too late!

Fiona Oliver

NATURE

ARCTIC DREAM

I had a nightmare, the polar icecaps had
completely disappeared,
Leaving gaps where once existed an
expanse, a chilly, icy land.
Polar bears looking lost, stranded on blocks
of floating ice,
as though waiting for some saviour to
suddenly appear -

rescue them, return them to their homeland
of permafrost,
back to life, scavenging on whale carcasses
and hunting seals,
As the glaciers of the arctic continents melt
into the ocean's depths,
due to global warming and human
selfishness, the deadly cost.

Childhood images of blue-white snows,
were my arctic dream,
A frigid tundra of cold, thick ice, creating
mountainous shapes,
Large, ominous icebergs, huge glaciers
crawling towards the icy sea,
Frozen landscapes forever lost, unless we
embrace being green.

Lis McDermott

WINTERS WALK

It isn't surprising, the world appears to be a friendly,
happier place when the sun shines upon your face.
Bright, blue skies are a welcome sight after weeks of
wintery, wet, gloomy days.

A short walk in the sunshine, breathing crisp, fresh
country air will surely blow the cobwebs away.
Wrap up warmly, the temperature's low, later
there could well be flurries of snow.

Morning mist has long dispersed, revealing fields
all blanketed in white, with a sparkling, frosty glow.
High in the sky, seagulls, black crows endlessly
circle, flying to and fro.

Icy patches remain at the side of the lane,
Where water has collected after
yesterday's rain.
The silence is deafening, apart from a
lowly
blackbird with bright yellow beak, singing
its sweet,
melodic refrain.

Hedgerows of thick hawthorn, prickly
brambles lay
dormant and bare,
Watch out for the cheeky, red robin who
resides there.
Lifeless trees line the way, exuding an air
of melancholy,
Mourning last year's story of autumn
glory.

Victims of lashing winter gales, dead
branches
litter all around, lying smashed, broken on
the ground.

Not one small creature, dormouse or
squirrel stir,
All are safely hidden away, in hollow
trees, or deep
inside burrows fast asleep, at this
freezing, desolate
time of the year.

Chilly north winds blow, turning thoughts
to
returning to the cosy comfort of sitting in
front
of a blazing log fire, thawing hands, toes,
feet,
luxuriating in the lovely heat.
Drinking frothy, hot chocolate,
What a delicious treat!

Carolyn Crawford

RED STORM DAY

Trees bend and creak, their branches
become flailing slaves
to the gusts of wind, blowing destruction
across the land.
The rushing wind mimics the crashing
sounds of waves,
as trampolines vault over fences; showing
off their handstands.

Abandoned dustbins bounce down the
street, causing mayhem.
leaving their contents liberally strewn in
other people's spaces.
'Didn't they watch or listen to the news last
night?' we all condemn,
as we watch them career along, missing
cars; terror on our faces.

Warmly wrapped against the forces,
snuggled with our hot drinks,
Listening to creaks, rattling, bangs outside,
expecting to hear roof-tiles fall.
Worried about costly repairs storm Eunice
is wreaking with her high jinks,
Anxiously, we wonder, what she'll destroy
with her next violent squall.

Lis McDermott

WINTER WALK

My pockets are a bulging mess
With Christmas chocolates, I confess.
My brand new wellies put up a fight
As I squeeze my shins in; they're so
tight

A winter walk sounded good
I can't believe I said I would
Walk six miles to reach the pub
God, my wellies really rub

I've climbed up gates and over fences
Waded through the flood defences
Slipped on moss and triple sulcoed
Wished I was in Acapulco

I've moaned and yelped and even cried
You said not much further, but you lied.
My feet are frozen, fingers blue
Still there's no pub within my view.

This winter walk is not much fun
I can't believe how far we've come
Our house is just a distant speck
And I'm a soggy, frozen wreck

My brand new water bottle, full of gin
Is empty now, and I want to sing
In fact it's the best fun that I've had
This winter walk is not so bad

I've finally made it to the pub
I think I'll join the Ramblers Club
But first I'll have a large hot toddy
And order myself a brand new body.

Fiona Oliver

WINTERS WALK

What spell do you cast that makes me
yearn?
For your visit where you will stay
For a week, or even a day or two
Before once more, you go away.

This ugly world that's all around
You can change in just one night
And make this dreary life of mine
Renewed and clean and bright.

But yet another day goes by
Vague promises that I believed
Tomorrow maybe, but not for sure…
But no, again I've been deceived

All day I waited longingly
Once more you did not show
Just mist and rain, a little sleet,
Not what I love, fresh fallen snow.

John Phillips

ARCTIC DREAMS

My name is Misha, I'm a polar bear.
I live here alone, not one of a pair.
I'm polar white, not custard cream,
And I've got a plan, an arctic dream.

I live in Bristol, but I want to be free,
To swim around in the ice cold sea.
I don't like living in a concrete zoo,
I want to be free, just like you.

I rock to and fro, while everyone stares.
I'm not one of the happiest bears.
A little girl cries with her mum and dad.
They know that I feel really sad.

I've got a dream, that I'll be freed one
day.
An arctic dream, that may come my
way.
No more painted white concrete floors,
Or high stone walls, with locked metal
doors.

I'm a polar bear and I'm brave and bold,
But I only thrive in the ice and the cold.
Imagine the miles of snow I will see,
If my dream comes true and I can be me.

Fiona Oliver

HER WINTER PALACE

White light pours through the darkness;
Outside fluffy snowflakes are falling.
The world is shrouded in feathery
whiteness;
Of ethereal beauty, and wonder enthralling.

Snowflakes flying in every direction,
Swirling upwards overhead.
A winter wonderland of glistening
perfection,
Awaits her, arising from her warm bed.

After the storm the whole world sparkles,
Even the winter sun shines brightly today.
Outside, an eerie air of silence startles,
As she rides out, aboard a one horse
open sleigh.

The merry sound of sleigh bells jingle
jangle
moving on, slip, sliding along.
Soft, white snow blankets the steep,
sloping
hillsides, rising up to greet the sky, all
around.
Freedom calls, far away from life's busy
throng.

Rays of dappled, bright sunshine fall through
snow clad pine trees, twinkling down to the snowy white ground.
Magically enhancing the glistening trees,
standing tall, regimentally row upon row.

The light is fading, the temperature is falling,
it's time to return.
Is it the cold, rushing wind, or the thrill of the
ride that has turned her face all aglow?
Faster, faster the horse gallops, no need for undue concern.

She longs for the warmth of a blazing log fire;
And the sound of her lively children at play.
Later in the evening they'll hear music played
by her favourite orchestral choir;
Warm and cosy, in their winter palace, at the
end of a fairytale kind of a day.

Carolyne Crawford

WINTER WALK

Out and about for my daily sojourn
my breath escapes, creating fog around;
This crisp season unto earth I was born;
Cracking twigs and birdsong the only
sound
as I trudge across the rock hardened
ground.
Met by skeletal trees, mulched leaf debris
as I wander through this eerie, mud-sea,
birdsong fills the wintery clear, bright blue
skies
My heart overflows, grateful to be free
in this worlds wondrous gift of nature's
prize.

Lis McDermott

ALL HALLOWS EVE

Twilight fell… a sinister spirit stirred,
Deep in the depths of the cold,
decomposing earth;
In the stillness not a sound could be heard.
Out of nowhere a chilling, dense mist
whirled and
swirled, shrouding the leafy glade.
Dark clouds gathered, thunder clapped,
lightning
flashed, arced across the sky's dark façade.
Devoid of all leaves, the wind whistled and
whined,
magnified through tall, imposing trees;
Time stood still, the temperature began to
freeze.
Small creatures hurried and scurried to hide
away
from the hideous, blood-curdling
cacophony of sound.
Tonight, beware the malevolent terror that
lurks,
stalking its prey in the murky, inky
blackness around;
On this ghastly, nightmarish, All Hallows'
Eve.

Carolyne Crawford

AUTUMN

Autumn season glimmers into sight,
Trees lose their gowns of gorgeous greens,
Nature's changes create glorious gems,
Jewels of embellished, foliage, enhancing
branches
In golds, yellows, burnt oranges, rich reds,
Riotous, colourful clusters of luscious
leaves,
Scattering as they fall, confetti, crisp,
crunchy,
Turning to gossamer, lace-like skeletons,
strewn
For us to gently tread as we traverse
carpeted pathways.

Lis McDermott

AUTUMN HAIKU

Autumn my favourite

Season of leaves and colour

Crimson red and death

Debra Pitchford

AUTUMNAL

An autumnal feel to the day, as leaves fall, scatter
beneath my feet, decorating my hair;
natures jewels.
Clothed for warmth, I survey this beautiful land; the
distant valley, asleep; ghostly sounds eerily echo,
early morning mist, shrouds a gradually
brightening sun.

Forests peter out into a line of trees, leading towards the
glow of the bright, gold dazzling morning sun, rising behind the
hills. Conversational sheep bleat their hearts desires to passing birds.
In a further field, like lemmings, sheep wander across the field,
jumping occasionally, performing their woolly line-dance.

Knightly guards, ancient trees stand midst damp, dewy fields,
leafless branches of the eldest, pointing aimlessly into the sky.

Morning awakes, humanity slowly appears,
as farmers traverse narrow country lanes to
care for their livestock, tend fields,
organically sow seeds, growing their crops.

Passing through this cornucopia of life, so
quintessentially British, I am grateful for
this land.
Relaxing into my constitutional, as early
mists lift,
stretching out before me lie hills and dales,
a whole
terrain nature-rich filled with sounds and
smells of the earth.

Under the sun, moon and stars, gritstone
ridges
vistas of stark moorlands and wetland
valleys,
we wend our way, traversing to the highest
peaks, but
xeric plants will not be found here. This
domain calls us
yearly to visit, walk, climb, take in the
sights and feel the
zephyr blowing against our bodies,
welcoming us home.

Lis McDermott

DANCING WITH DANDELIONS

It's been a gloriously warm Spring day;
With promise of summer happiness not far
away.
As the sun sinks gracefully into the west,
It's time for the world of humans to take
their
peaceful rest.
By the light of the silvery moon, in a
meadow
filled with golden dandelions, flower
fairies gather
for the Dandelion Ball tonight.
Eager woodland creatures await the first
sighting
of their magical fairy light.
At the stroke of midnight the air resounds
to the
echo of fluttering fairy wings;
In a flash a multitude of flower fairies fly
in.
Daintily adorned in fine gossamer dress,
with tiny
petal hats of roses, marigolds, pansies,
orchids.
All land together to a rousing cheer;

Followed by fairy snowdrops, bluebells, daisies,
daffodils bringing up the rear.
At the shrill hoot of an owl celebrations begin.
Fairies dance, fly with abandon amongst the
dandelions, swishing, swirling round and round
in an endless spin.
By special request a flock of shy nightingales
start to beautifully sing;
Accompanied by the steady rhythmic humming
of birds on the wing.
The flower fairies dance on late into the night;
It's difficult to imagine a more splendiferous sight.
Exhilarated, energised after long winter's hibernation,
they await the call of Mother Nature to assist in the
perfection of her new designer, floral summer creation.

At the crack of dawn all lay quiet, serene,
Except through the mist a profusion of
ghostly, fluffy,
grey parachute-like dandelion seeds
disperse, drifting
upon the breeze, adding magic afresh to the
early
morning scene.

Carolyne Crawford

AUTUMN

On the swirling autumn wind, leaves softly
fall
Curls of smoke gently twirl from
chimneys, standing tall
Trees shed their golden glow, leaving
branches bare.
On the hob, home-made soup, almost ready
to share
Blanket frosts paint the landscape sparkly
white,
Early birds preparing for their long winter
flight
Revelling in the embers of the fading
Autumn light.

Fiona Oliver

DANDELIONS

Tip toe through the tulips
Is how the song should go.
But oh, my dear, what is so wrong
Tip-toeing thro' dandelions as they grow.

We always think of them as weeds
And yet they are so strong.
For every year they keep returning
To create another sunny song.

And so with care, and light of feet,
I'll cross the verdant grass.
And dance amongst the dandelions
Cause tulips never last.

Ann Brady

FUCHSIA SMILES

Their heads hang down as if bowing
But it is only just their way
For they are meant to bring you joy
00No matter the sort of day

They come in many colours
Their trumpets make no sound
The petals open like a double cloak
Spreading a delightful scent around

The colours come in shades of pink,
reds, purples, and even white.
They make your garden shimmer
What a glorious, colourful sight.

And as I look at the Fuchsias,
staring at them for a while.
I enjoy their wide varieties
for they have always make me smile.

Ann Brady

STILL I RISE

Despite the lack of care for my fate,
Still I rise.
Too many nations ignore my cries,
as heat soars at an alarming rate.

Though talk about a global mandate,
levels of my oceans reach new highs.
Despite the lack of care for my fate,
Still I rise.

Humans must act before it's too late.
Forest fires burn, darken once blue skies,
animals extinct, their genus dies.
Naïve, you, your own death-wish will
narrate.
Despite the lack of care for my fate,
 Still I rise.

Lis McDermott

THE SEA

When your soul needs to heal,
Make your way to the sea
It's magic; you'll see!
Your face soft with sea spray
lips tasting brine
Breathe in the sea air
As you walk the long bay.
Your Feet made for splashing
Along the shoreline.
Your ears primed to listen
To distant waves crashing.
Your eyes to view water
that flickers and glistens.
Breathe in the sea air
Feel your heart beam.
Your senses all tuned,
primed and attuned.
The sea it is magical,
It transcends the physical.
So, when you need to heal
Go to the sea
Be healed,
and renew your life's zeal

Debra Pitchford

GLOBAL WARMING

Small, winged seeds rise, gain flight,
float on an invisible breeze up into the
dirty,
smoggy air.
Come to land in a once verdant field now
dry,
dusty, barren and bare.
In this desolate place does anyone care?
The seeds are the only hope for new life on
the
scorched, over-heating, dying earth;
They require nutrients, water for rebirth.

All is quiet, in the silence not one bird can
be
seen or heard.
There are no animals left, insects, or bees;
For no vegetation remains for creatures to
feed.
Temperatures soar as carbon emissions
rise;

Humanity can barely survive; hunger, drought,
extreme weather comes as no surprise.
In the future, hopefully this doomsday scenario
won't become a catastrophic reality.

Time is growing short, if we all stopped being
complacent positive steps could be taken to call
a halt to our planet's fragility.
At the moment efforts to stem global warming
seem a shameful travesty.
For the sake of generations to come, society
must take full responsibility and unite.
It's now or never, we must cherish our beautiful
world; nurture, protect it from this perilous plight.

Carolyne Crawford

IN THE FOREST

It's an early summer's morning and the
forest
glade presents a tranquil scene;
At this moment all lay silent, still and
serene.
A fresh breeze stirs through tall, spreading
chestnut trees:
The first dappled rays of sunlight cascade
down
through large, green leaves:
Fragile spider's webs sparkle and glisten
when the morning dew falls wet to the
ground:
Birds awaken, vanquishing the silence
with their sweet, melodic sound:
Small creatures hurry and scurry,
foxes return from hunting to their lair:
Strutting pigeons bill and coo, flying into
the air:
Close-by a thirsty deer drinks from the
ferny banks
of a pebbly stream;

The trickling water flows pure and clean.
In this out of the way place the circle of
life
continues, day after day.
A far cry away from the warring world of
today.
It may seem mundane, but all is just as it
should
be, in this wild and wonderful country
domain

Carolyne Crawford

SPRINGTIME

Winter blues turn to joyful hope of brighter
times ahead;
As Spring days become longer.
Delicate, white snowdrops with cute capped
heads push through cold earth, slowly rising
from their winter's bed;
When the sun's rays become stronger.
Sunny, yellow daffodils shoot up to reach the sky,
Heads swaying in a merry dance, frilly trumpets all
aglow, heralding a sublime Springtime extravaganza.
Hedgerows awake bringing forth a multi-coloured
show, that will delight the eye of every passer-by,
Freely offering a spectacular floral bonanza.

Spring fever takes hold, trees that blossom look
pretty in pink.
Birds once again sweetly sing;
Flying to and fro, building nests all in sync.
Mood lightens as days brighten, it feels good to be
alive, to embrace the resplendent glory of the rebirth
of blooming Spring.

Carolyne Crawford

MY GARDEN

A garden is a creation in musical art.
It sings out in shades of harmonious colour,
like an emotive ballad, sung straight from
the heart
An enchanting palette of sweet fragrant
notes
float gently on an ayre, for senses to
discover.
An evolving composition, is a garden's key
changing mission.
A gardener's quest is to orchestrate and
conduct,
through all the seasons in ceaseless
repetition,
mollified and charmed by the garden's
soulful rendition.

Debra Pitchford

MY POTTING SHED

My potting shed
is the place to escape,
away from the house,
a quiet place to be -

With shelves full of pots
and tubs full of seed,
and a resident mouse,
who is as quiet as can be.

My potting shed
is where seeds start to grow,
set to plant in my garden
all neatly laid in rows.

My potting shed,
my quiet place to be,
has a window, dusty and cracked,
Nothing is perfect- that's a fact.

My potting shed
is where, without reason
I can pause whilst drinking tea,

Quietly gaze at my garden,
Feeling proud as can be.

Debra Pitchford

DEEP IN DARKNESS

Deep in darkness down below,
Watch and wait for a miracle to unfold.
From tiny seeds, pretty plants will
grow.
For now, all lay dormant, fast asleep,
enduring winter snow and cold.

In springtime when the sun awakes,
The rich, dark earth will stir and warm.
April showers, warmth is all it takes
for healthy, green shoots to sprout and
form.

Growing taller and taller by the day,
Rising to greet the bright blue sky.
Like any other job, it's a labour of love
to keep the weeds at bay.
Tend and water regularly, don't let the
plants grow leggy, too high.

In a short time, buds will begin to
bloom,
bursting forth into flower, producing a
startling show.
Smell the fragrant scent of their
perfume,

As you laze beneath the grand canopy of
a tall, trailing weeping willow.

Carolyne Crawford

DISCUSSION

BEING A MISFIT

I've often wondered what I am?
And do I really fit?
Are you able to understand
The reality of being a misfit?

Cause that is what I think I am
I've never really conformed.
Always going down my own path,
proudly blowing my own horn.

But when I look around this world
It's not that I don't fit.
I'm beginning now to feel the norm
'Cause everyone else is also a misfit.

Ann Brady

IS THERE A RULE OF ANARCHY?

You walk the path only you can choose.
Regardless of any others.
Your freedom gained is only at
the suffering of your brothers.
You do not care about right or wrong.
For in your faith you think and
believe that you are strong.
And yet, when something does not go your
way,
who will you find to make them pay?
For it is in your stupid foolishness,
stubborn minds, and crazy mulishness,
that will lead you down the path to doom;
eventually towards your resting tomb.
Do not believe in anarchy,
for the rule of anarchy is not a rule.
Unless, of course, you are as dumb
and as stupid as the mule!

Ann Brady

IF WE ALL STOPPED

Scared of things we don't understand,
wary of people from other lands;
They'd receive better receptions,
if we all stopped making
perceptions.

Oft living in different conditions,
with other religious traditions.
We could quash our growing conceptions
if we all stopped making
perceptions.

A world where we could live side by side,
Let bias, bigotry be denied,
Open our hearts, push out objections,
if we all stopped making
perceptions.

Lis McDermott

I TRIED!

I honestly tried to help her, as I knew she needed it so.

But how was I to really know, that her mind was twisted with such woe.

Her emails had been full of anger, a vitriolic avalanche.

So why did she suddenly turn on me, when I'd only offered her an olive branch.

And so I feel great sadness, that fills my heart quite deep.

How can we guess what others will send, in their emails after you have gone to sleep?

Ann Brady

ENOUGH

Is it enough,
to raise your children to be carefree,
without reminding them about
responsibility?

Is it enough,
that our governments are in control
just because they won a political poll?

Is it enough,
for them to make all the laws and rules,
then not follow them, making us into fools?

Is it enough,
when the world's leaders meet up for the
G8 summit
yet our overall care of the earth continues
to plummet?

Is it enough,
the help we give to those living in poverty;
still on the rise,
whilst others are overwhelmed with riches
and supplies?

Is it enough,
with so many wars, world statesmen
negotiate for peace,
but only if supporting their views, do they
want them to cease.

Is it enough?
That is the question; the ongoing,
important task
is to keep searching for answers and
continually ask;
Is it enough?

Lis McDermott

ENOUGH

I might not have a full set of teeth,
Or wear a bra with matching briefs!
I might not be a svelte size ten,
Or have a personal trainer called Sven!
But I'm enough.

I might not be a domestic goddess
Or cope well with a household crisis!
I might not cook a brilliant meal,
Or get the best energy deal!
But I'm enough

I might not clearly say what I mean,
Or remember exactly where I've been!
I might not always get it exactly right,
I may have missed the odd train or flight!
But I'm enough.

I might not remember a special date,
And I know I'm very often late!
I might get distracted, lose the plot
And the menopause makes me really hot!
But I'm enough.

I might spend too much time alone,
Pondering how to lose at least two stone!
I might need to tell myself, I'm enough,
Rather than worrying about all the stupid
stuff!
Because I am, enough!

Fiona Oliver

STANDING STILL

I pondered on the question
If we should stop and stare
What would become of today
If no-one really cared.

If every person just stood still
And never blinked an eye
Would we stop breathing in and out?
Would we all just up and die?

Perhaps we should, just for a mo'
Think about this world.
For of it stopped rotating around
Then we'd all end up underground.

Ann Brady

PRISONER

I am not guilty of a crime
Though sentenced now to serve some time,
Judgement is passed the term is life
He owns me now, I am his wife.

To cook and clean, a common slave
Fulfilling all that he may crave,
And live in fear when he is annoyed
All that I was, he has destroyed.

He tells me of the clothes to wear,
And makes me cover up my hair,
Who I talk to, who I can see
It is no longer up to me.

I have his babies, one a year
Sometimes the pains too much to bear.
Existing only for his pleasure
To abuse or use, in equal measure.

When I'm used up he'll find another
To ensure his children have a mother,
Sentence is passed, the term is life
I no longer exist, I am just his wife.

John Phillips

SUNFLOWERS

The Russian soldier entered her city
A Ukrainian woman showed him pity
She let him use her mobile phone
So he could call his mama, at home
He sobbed with shame for what he'd done,
Comforted by strangers, he lay down his
gun.

Other soldiers, given sunflower seeds,
By an elderly woman, who gently pleads
'Take these with you, for when you fall,
These bright yellow flowers will grow tall,
And mark the place you took your last
breath,
An eternal reminder of your death.

Sons and daughters, sent by old men
To fight a war they cannot win.
Killed with kindness, filled with shame,
Murdering civilians, children slain.
Blood on their hands, on their face
War is the scourge of the human race.

Fiona Oliver

PERSONAL ZONE

SILENCE SOUNDED LIKE...

Silence sounded like...
>A sleeping child
>Newly born today.

Silence sounded like...
>The calm sea breeze
>Making the waves gently sway.

Silence sounded like...
>A tolling bell now sitting still
>It's echo long since passed.

Silence sounded like...
>The moment you took
>Your long final breath.

Silence is something we often wish for
>Yet at other times we don't.

Silence sounded like…
        Anything you wish for
        As long as you are in it.

Silence sounded like…
        Silence….

Ann Brady

THE QUIET ZONE

It's hot and humid, this sunny day,
I've used google maps to find my way.
My Fitbit thinks that it's been stolen,
So many steps, my feet are swollen.

I've finally found my Waterloo,
The stations there, it's in my view.
The departure board says gate nine,
If I run, I'll get there in time.

Front 3 carriages for my stop,
I really think I'm fit to drop.
People standing, there's no seats,
I can't bear it! My poor feet!

But then, I see an empty space.
I make my way, indecent haste.
Wild eyed and reckless, I fight through,
That space is mine, it's my pew.

No one dares to block my way,
I've got that look - 'get out my way'.
I swing into the empty seat with glee,
This is the perfect place for me.

I want to cheer and celebrate,
And then I see the sign I hate.
No music, talking or use of phones!
I'm in the bloody quiet zone.

Fiona Oliver

WHAT HAPPENED TO YOUR WINGS?

You used to be so proud and confident
Always at the centre of attention; the main
event
Yet, today you are curiously listless and
quiet,
Your brilliance lost, as though on a silence
diet.
What happened to your wings?

Once the life and soul of the party,
a winner, always totally hale and hearty.
Have you lost your faith and joyous esprit?
Where is your pizzazz and quick repartee?
always at the ready to give that sarcastic
reply.
Did you really believe you could fly?

I am sorry you are feeling so sad and low,
Having been pulled down by the undertow.
A sprinkling of humility should be owned
by all.

The closer to the sun you fly, the further you'll fall…
Is that what happened to your wings?

Lis McDermott

JACK BE NIMBLE

Very short history. Traditionally fire leaping was practised at English fairs, but was eventually banned due to the danger, being replaced with candle leaping.
Also ref. a pirate named Jack Black, who had to be quick (nimble) to escape capture.

* * * * *

The story says Jack was quite nimble
It also said he was quick
But Jack was neither, he was clumsy as
hell
And well known as a bit of a dick

A village custom for all their young men
Was leaping over a large burning pyre
But Jack always failed this perilous task
Most times with his ass caught on fire

Some of his friends would encourage him

Shouting 'this time you can do it our Jack'

Although they all knew he would once
again fail
While he kept smoking that poisonous
crack

Disappointed again in the way he'd
performed
So in shame one night crept away
I love this village and all of my friends
And vow to come back here one day

When that day came all of his friends asked
Jack please tell us where you have been
I have spent a long time in a rehab house
And now I am three months clean

My head is also so clear now
And I know I am still not too quick
But I will leap over a burning flame
Though only one in a large candlestick.

John Phillips

THE COST OF PLAGARISM

'I wandered lonely as a cloud
That floats on high o'er vales and hills'

But these words seem familiar to me, did
someone else write them,
and they are a faint memory that I am
recalling?
I think I will go for a walk
to clear my head before writing anymore.

 I had been walking for about an hour

 'when all at once I saw
a host of golden daffodils.'

Well, not so much a crowd, or host, but
quite
a lot,
But I still have this nagging feeling that I
have read
something like this years ago. So, I found a
nice place to sit down and contemplate,

'Beside the lake, beneath the trees
Fluttering and dancing in the breeze'

I wondered, even if I accidently use something that has been written by somebody else, and
They sue me. What would it cost? Would it be the cost of a paragraph, a page or even a Syllable?

Or maybe they would just charge me for whatever a Wordsworth.

John Phillips

AM I REDUNDANT?

Am I redundant? Am I obsolete
just taking up another seat?
It must be true as I'm sometimes told
"You have no use now that you're old"

What knowledge I have no longer matters
As my girls believe my brain's in tatters
They treat their granny like a new-born
baby
And make me wear a Tena Lady

I know I no longer move as fast
Not like I used to in the past
But for decades I've been on my own
So, don't dare mention, nursing home

I notice often when you glance at me
And think "my god that look could kill"
But you still have to be nice, for a little
while
As it's never too late to change my will.

John Phillips

BETRAYED

Oh, the treachery of a solitary tear
As my sorrow I try to hide,
Reveals my innermost feelings, I fear
All those I seek to keep inside.

It glistens briefly on my cheek
I cannot make it stop,
My secret self I wish to keep
Exposed in just a single drop.

Revealing more than I care to share
Unmasked an image that I hold dear,
Destroying my pride that I proudly wear
Oh, the treachery of a solitary tear.

John Phillips

NO LATE FLIGHTS

Late night flight
No front lights.
Fumbling in handbag
Dropping the flight bag
Contents fallout
Keys join breakout.

Hands gathering
So much clattering
Key Fob knocking
Door unlocking
a dooshbag,
with jet lag!

Bag slinging
Door swinging
Silence broken.
Household woken.
The creak on the stair?
Too late to care

Debra Pitchford

A CHRISTMAS COUNTDOWN

Hurray, only five sleeps 'til Christmas Day.
At last school has broken up until next
year.
The dreaded nativity play is over and done,

after tantrums and a few tears.
I was glad when the last carol was sung.
This year Mum, Dad, Grandma came
along.
They said I shone brightly, I was the best
angel
Gabriel they'd ever seen.
For a change I'd stood still, looked
angelic,
sweet, serene.
Mum sent teacher a box of chocolates, as a
gift for putting up with me.
To make amends for when I fell head first
into
the school's Christmas tree.

Only 4 sleeps 'til Christmas.
Christmas excitement is bubbling, my mind
is
whirring, I just can't wait for the start of
family fun.

Mum says I need to calm down, as festivities have
only just begun.
She's given me lots of boring jobs to do, in the
fond hope they will help,
But I'd rather be playing games on my tablet, or
watching pirate movies starring Johnny Depp.

Only 3 sleeps 'til Christmas.
Oh joy! Mum has dragged me with her to do the
last minute shopping in the freezing weather today.
The car park is full, the shops are over-crowded,
she's snappy, stressed, seems to be in total disarray.
I'd better be good, perhaps I'll perform my famous
disappearing act when the time comes to put the
shopping away.

Only two sleeps 'til Christmas.
The house is looking festive, decorated with holly,
mistletoe.
A copy of the Radio Times lays ready, waiting for us
to choose our favourite Christmas show.
The fridge and freezer are bulging with all Mum's
yummy party food delights,
Sadly, she's hidden all the nuts and chocolates
out of reach and sight.

Nearly there, only one sleep to go.
Mum is frantically stuffing the turkey, peeling
vegetables, preparing yucky Bru56ssel sprouts.

I'm hiding in my bedroom away from all her
frantic,
panicking shouts.
All is well, she is singing carols, eating mince pies,
her glass full to overflowing with sparkly, bubbly

Christmas Eve fizz.
Dad's an absolute star, a technological whizz,
He's set up an App to track Santa's toy laden sleigh,
I can watch it if I go to bed without delay.
What a relief to know he's finally on his way.
God, please bless Santa to arrive safe and sound tonight,
Make our Christmas Day merry and bright.

Carolyne Crawford

ITS LIKE A GOOD-FITTING GLOVE

Fetching the mail after the postman has called.
Wondering how much he has left in the hall.
Where do the letters and postcards come from?
Is it America, Australia, or maybe Sierra Leone?

It doesn't really matter who has written to me.
Because all I ever want is some writing to see.
Those words that are written on the paper so neat
are ecstatic to me, such a powerful treat.

The words enter my mind, being almost biblical.
I devour and absorb each letter and syllable.
Where did we learn this craft so delightful?
Of placing down squiggles that charm, or are spiteful.

We write with gay abandon, a mindset full
of determination.
Never worrying or caring about correct
punctuation.
And when we are done, our words are
concluded,
finished at last, as we no longer feel
secluded.

Into an envelope, we entrust our thoughts
and dreams.
It's all meant to be part of that ever-larger
scheme.
Sharing our views, our fears, and our love,
writing for me, is like wearing a good-
fitting glove.

Ann Brady

AND STILL I RISE

Loved before my first gasp of air,
By parents who showed me so much care,
'Dream big and reach for the skies'
They believe, and still I rise.

My maths teacher thought me slow,
When my numbers simply would not flow.
She pursed her lips, she rolled her eyes,
She was wrong, and still I rise.

My first boss threw a stapler at my head,
I ducked, it hit the door instead.
He was a bully, and not very wise
He was weak, and still I rise.

By twenty, I was married, happy as can be
To a husband I believe in and who believes
in me.
I am a married woman, with stars in my
eyes
I am loved, and still I rise.

My body bears four babies, only three
survived.
To be the best of mothers, I have always
strived.
A working mother, despite the sighs,
I learn to juggle, and still I rise.

My family are grown, my job is done,
I've worked hard and had some fun.
I can't believe how quickly time flies,
I'm fifty-five, and still I rise.

Just when you think you've hit the top,
You realise you have no time to stop.
A grand-daughter arrives, a great surprise
A new life to learn from, and still I rise.
I rise, I rise, I rise

Fiona Oliver

POETS INFORMATION, AND THE PAGES THEIR POETRY APPEARS.

Ann Brady is a published author, a writer's mentor, a publisher, and a part-time poet. The latter she does for fun. She is based in Cardiff and has published a range of books, including an award-winning historical novel, a children's picture book series, plus a variety of other genres. She mentors' writers of all ages and has published several books written by younger writers.

www.ann-brady.co.uk

www.mentoringwriters.co.uk

Poetry Pages: **13, 14, 22, 42, 48, 52, 61, 94, 95, 110, 111, 113, 118, 122, 139**

Carolyne Crawford was born (b. 1950) and raised in Middlesbrough, in the North-East of England. She now lives in Wiltshire with her husband, two daughters, and six grandsons.

After a successful secretarial career in banking, and law, she worked for the Personnel Department of a famous French

Perfumery House, retiring early, to take golf lessons and to became a golfing addict. She is a nature lover, being especially passionate about her garden, plays Bridge, dabbles in watercolour painting, and is an avid reader of all genres. With no previous writing experience, she wrote her first poem 7 years ago, taking inspiration from her Christian faith. Carolyne feels blessed to have joined Lis' Poetry Group of talented poets and hopes to continue writing, reading, and enjoying poetry for the foreseeable future

Poetry Pages: **18, 39, 44, 50, 54, 57, 73, 82, 85, 90, 98, 100, 102, 106, 135**

Lis McDermott, who started the poetry group, is a published author and poet. She is based in Wiltshire, where she lives with her husband. After a successful career in music education, where she worked for 34 years, she started her own photography business, working for 12 years. Lis began writing seriously in 2017 and now works as a writing mentor. She has published a range of books, including short stories, an autobiography, four poetry books, and her first novel, published in 2022.

www.LisMcDermottAuthor.co.uk

Poetry Pages: **7, 24, 37, 46, 72, 76, 84, 86, 88, 96, 112, 114, 126**

Fiona Oliver is a Charity CEO from South Wiltshire. Despite having the best job in the world, and an all-round fabulous family and friends, life is sometimes very stressful and it is at those times that poetry saves the day! So, rather than going to the gym or a therapist, Fiona tries to write poetry that will make her and others laugh. This has not made her any thinner but it has certainly made her a lot happier!

Poetry Pages: **6, 8, 12, 56, 63, 65, 66, 68, 77, 80, 93, 116, 120, 124, 141**

John Phillips, a Welshman born and bred, retired ten years ago after a career as a Clinical Hypnotherapist and Counsellor. He has since been able to pursue his passion for writing. His children's books have been published under the pen name of

Sebastian Stumblebum. But, as he can be somewhat cynical of society's failure to care for our planet, he deemed that his adult fiction, and environmental stories that have a sometimes-sarcastic edge, best published under his alter ego of Lawrence Dracut. Poetry is yet another side to his multifaceted personality.

Poetry Pages: **16, 25, 27, 28, 30, 32, 34, 38, 59, 79, 119, 128, 130, 132, 133**

Debra Pitchford is a Learning and Development Consultant with a passion for hiking and the great outdoors. She and her husband share their home in the beautiful Forest of Dean in Gloucestershire with their son, a menagerie of animals, and a lifetime collection of books.

Debra started writing poems to accompany her photographic work, before beginning to experiment with poetry about people, and life in general.

Poetry Pages: **36, 87, 97, 104, 105, 134**

If you are interested in joining **Lis' Poetry Place**, please contact her on:

Lis@lismcdermottauthor.co.uk

Read more about the group at:

https://lismcdermottauthor.co.uk/poetry-place.html

Book Published by:

Pen & Ink Designs Publishing

www.penandinkdesigns.co.uk

www.ingramcontent.com/pod-product-compliance
Lightning Source LLC
Chambersburg PA
CBHW042337040426
42447CB00017B/3459